T0193637

It's a Dad's Thing

PART 3 - THE CRAZY DAD

ADAM ATCHA

Balboa Press books may be ordered through booksellers or by contacting:

Balboa Press
A Division of Hay House
1663 Liberty Drive
Bloomington, IN 47403
www.balboapress.com.au
AU TFN: 1 800 844 925 (Toll Free inside Australia)
AU Local: 0283 107 086 (+61 2 8310 7086 from outside Australia)

ISBN: 978-1-5043-2301-7 (sc)
ISBN: 978-1-5043-2302-4 (e)

Print information available on the last page.

Balboa Press rev. date: 10/21/2020

BALBOAPRESS
A DIVISION OF HAY HOUSE

A Stupid Dad gives up on Her/
Him without any Understanding

A Revengeful Dad
pretends to Love them

A Hateless Dad hears no
Evil and Sees no Evil
Unconsciously – Creepy

An Awesome Dads engages
in all Relationships with
or without Them,

A Mentally Ill Dad wants
Reignition in fact to Impress
lesser and Love Morer

A Stay Home Dad suffers

like a Mother —

An Abused Father is Frightened
of all their actions weather
Positive or Negative –

A Great Dad Simply Cares and
Loves all Unconditionally,

A Friendly Dad is also a
Proud Father and Respected
in His Community –

An alcoholic Dad has High
Morals and Values and looks
down at Himself —

A Heartless Dad makes no Sense
yet is Possible Sometimes —

Our Father is the One who
give us The Strength, Courage
to do Better Every day.

It is not Possible to live without
a Dad by Hating Him –

A Hard-Working Father
loves her/him by the Shelter
he provides for Them

A Notorious Father trains
Them in Self Defence —

A Diplomatic Dad loves
everything and anything When
he puts His Mind to it,

An Unfaithful Dad…

A Generous Father gives his
offspring's Everything He owns —

A Suburban Dad Cannot Boast,

Printed in the United States
By Bookmasters